Handy Wyoming Genealogy Handbook

Gary L. Morris

©2015 Gary L. Morris

ISBN-13: 978-1507866924

ISBN-10: 1507866925

Table of Contents

Notes

Genealogical Research in Wyoming

There is a wealth of genealogical records and resources available for tracing your family history in Wyoming. Because of the abundance of information held at many different locations, tracking down the records for your ancestor can be an ominous task. Don't worry though, we know just where they are, and we'll show you which records you'll need, while helping you to understand:

1. What they are
2. Where to find them
3. How to use them

These records can be found both online and off, so we'll introduce you to online websites, indexes and databases, as well as brick-and-mortar repositories and other institutions that will help with your research in Wyoming. So that you will have a more comprehensive understanding of these records, we have provided a brief history of the "Cowboy State" to illustrate what type of records may have been generated during specific time periods. That information will assist you in pinpointing times and locations on which to focus the search for your Wyoming ancestors and their records.

A Brief History of Wyoming

The forebears of the Native Americans who resided in Wyoming when the first Europeans arrived probably came by way of the Bering Strait and then ventured south. The first Europeans to explore Wyoming were French Canadian traders, namely the Vérendrye brothers, Louis-Joseph and Francois, who most likely reached the Big Horn Mountains in 1743, but moved on without laying claim to the area.

It wasn't until John Colter, an American fur trader, traversed most of the northwestern part of the state between 1806 and 1807, that any interest in the area was generated. Colter's reports of the beauty, probably including Yellowstone Park, fueled interest in the area, and subsequently many settlers passing through via the Oregon Trail decided to remain in Wyoming. Before the discovery of gold in California in 1848, travel on the Oregon Trail was minimal, but after the discovery a flood of "forty-niners" passed through the state.

Supply points along the Oregon Trail were established at Fort Bridger in the west and Ft. Laramie in the east, though few travelers remained in these areas. What finally brought serious settlers to the region was the completion of the Union Pacific Railroad, and towns such as Laramie, Rawlings, Cheyenne, and Rock Springs sprang up along the railway path. Wyoming was made a territory in 1868, and became the first state or territory to pass a women's suffrage act, doing so in 1869.

What Indian resistance to settlement existed was subdued before the end of the 1870's, and Wyoming became a center for cattlemen. Cattle barons dominated the land and the political sphere, and smaller ranches and cattle businesses were thwarted in their attempts to compete. The fight between the barons and small ranchers culminated in the so-named Johnson County War of 1891–92, in which the large landowners were arrested by government troops following attempts to take the law into their own hands.

Wyoming was made a state in 1890, but growth continued at a slow rate. Farming endeavors proved unsuccessful in this high, arid region, and Wyoming still remains a sparsely settled ranching state. The growth that has occurred has been mainly through the minerals industry, especially the development of oil, coal, and natural gas resources during the 1970s. The world's oil glut in the early 1980s slowed the growth of the state's energy industries however, and in 1984, non-fuel industry growth rates slowed as well.

Important Genealogical Dates in Wyoming History

1803 – Part of Louisiana Purchase

1834 – Fort Laramie and Fort Bridger established

1851 – Fort Laramie Treaty council held with plains and mountain tribes

1861 – Part of Dakota Territory

1867 – Gold Discovered at South Pass

1868 – Created as separate territory

1890 – Statehood

Famous Battles Fought in Wyoming

There have not been any great military battles fought in Wyoming, but there were numerous skirmished between white settlers and Native Americans during the formative years. The Legends of America website has a comprehensive listing of Wyoming **Indian War Battles, Skirmishes & Massacres.**

Indian War Battles, Skirmishes & Massacres : http://www.legendsofamerica.com/wy-indianbattles.html

The battle accounts that exist can be very effective in uncovering the military records of your ancestor. They can tell you what regiments fought in which battles, and often include the names and ranks of many officers and enlisted men.

Common Wyoming Genealogical Issues and Resources to Overcome Them

Boundary Changes: Boundary changes are a common obstacle when researching Wyoming ancestors. You could be searching for an ancestor's record in one county when in fact it is stored in a different one due to historical county boundary changes.

The **Atlas of Historical County Boundaries** can help you to overcome that problem. It provides a chronological listing of every boundary change that has occurred in the history of Wyoming.

Atlas of Historical County Boundaries:
http://publications.newberry.org/ahcbp/documents/WY_Consolidate d_Chronology.htm#Consolidated_Chronology

Name Changes: Surname changes, variations, and misspellings can complicate genealogical research. It is important to check all spelling variations. Soundex, a program that indexes names by sound, is a useful first step, but you can't rely on it completely as some name variations result in different Soundex codes. The surnames could be different, but the first name may be different too. You can also find records filed under initials, middle names, and nicknames as well, so you will need to **get creative with surname variations** and spellings in order to cover all the possibilities. For help with surname variations read our instructional article on **How to Use Soundex**.

get creative with surname variations:
http://obituarieshelp.org/blog/?p=634

How to Use Soundex: http://obituarieshelp.org/blog/?p=505

Wyoming Genealogical Organizations and Archives

Genealogical resources include not only records, but the organizations that house them, or can direct you to them. These institutions include: *Archives, Libraries, Genealogical Societies, Family History Centers, Universities, Churches, and Museums.*

Following are links to their websites, their physical addresses, and a summary of the records you can find there.

Archives and Libraries

Wyoming State Archives – Vital records, maps, newspapers, oral histories, school records, court records, cemetery listings, city directories, probate records, deeds, census records, military records, business records

2301 Central Avenue
Cheyenne, WY 82002
Telephone: 307-777-7826
Fax: 307-777-7044

Wyoming State Archives:
http://wyoarchives.state.wy.us/Archives/Genealogical.aspx

National Archives at Denver - Federal population censuses for all States, 1790-1930, Revolutionary War records, Pension and bounty land warrant applications, Ship's passenger lists, Indian censuses

17101 Huron Street
Broomfield, CO 80023
Telephone: 303-604-4740
Fax: 303-407-5707

National Archives at Denver:
http://www.archives.gov/denver/public/genealogy.html

Laramie County Library - Books and periodicals, state, county and town histories, probate, land, cemetery, church and vital records, federal census indexes, Family histories, military records and publications of American historical societies, including the Massachusetts Vital Records, the Rhode Island Vital Records, the War of the Rebellion series and the American Genealogical and Biographical Index

2200 Pioneer Avenue
Cheyenne, WY 82001
Telephone: 307-634-3561
Fax: 307-634-2082
Genealogy & Special Collections: 307-773-7232

Laramie County Library: http://www.lclsonline.org/

Wyoming State Library – Historical maps, newspapers, obituaries index, Ancestry and Heritage Quest

2800 Central Ave
Cheyenne, WY 82002-0006
Telephone: 307-777-6333
Fax: 307-777-6289

Wyoming State Library: http://gowyld.net/genealogy.html

University of Wyoming Library – Huge collection of genealogical and historical resources

Dept 3334
1000 E. University Ave
Laramie, WY 82071-3334
Telephone: 307-766-3190
Fax: 307-766-3062

University of Wyoming Library: http://www-lib.uwyo.edu/

Genealogical and Historical Societies

Genealogical and historical societies have access to extensive catalogues of genealogical data. They are also able to offer expert guidance for genealogical researchers. Many members are professional genealogists who are most willing to share their expertise in finding ancestors.

Cheyenne Genealogical & Historical Society – Excellent collection of resources for tracing Wyoming ancestry

P.O. Box 2539
Cheyenne, WY 82003-2539

Cheyenne Genealogical & Historical Society:
http://cghswyoming.org/main_page.html

Jackson Hole Historical Society and Museum
225 N. Cache St.
Jackson, WY 83001
Tel: (307) 733-2414
research@jacksonholehistory.org

Mailing Address:

P. O. Box 1005
Jackson, WY 83001

Jackson Hole Historical Society and Museum:
http://www.jacksonholehistory.org/

Sheridan Genealogical Society
P. O. Box 4075
Sheridan, WY 82801

Sheridan Genealogical Society:
http://www.rootsweb.ancestry.com/

Wyoming Mailing Lists

Mailing lists are internet based facilities that use email to distribute a single message to all who subscribe to it. When information on a particular surname, new records, or any other important genealogy information related to the mailing list topic becomes available, the subscribers are alerted to it. Joining a mailing list is an excellent way to stay up to date on Wyoming genealogy research topics. Rootsweb have an extensive listing of **Wyoming Mailing Lists** on a variety of topics.

Wyoming Mailing Lists:
http://lists.rootsweb.ancestry.com/index/usa/WY/misc.html

Wyoming Message Boards

A message board is another internet based facility where people can post questions about a specific genealogy topic and have it answered by other genealogists. If you have questions about a surname, record type, or research topic, you can post your question and other researchers and genealogists will help you with the answer. Be sure to check back regularly, as the answers are not emailed to you. The Wyoming message boards at **Rootsweb** are completely free to use.

Rootsweb:
http://boards.rootsweb.com/localities.northam.usa.states/mb.ashx

Wyoming Newspapers and Periodicals

Many genealogy periodicals and historical newspapers contain reprinted copies of family genealogies, transcripts of family Bible records, information about local records and archives, census indexes, church records, queries, land records, obituaries, court records, cemetery records, and wills. The following sites have historical Wyoming newspapers and periodicals that you can search online or on-site.

Wyoming State Archives – Most complete collection of Wyoming newspapers in existence from 1867 to the present.

2301 Central Avenue
Cheyenne, WY 82002
Telephone: 307-777-7826
Fax: 307-777-7044

Wyoming State Archives:
http://wyoarchives.state.wy.us/Archives/Genealogical.aspx

GenealogyBank.com – free searchable database of Wyoming newspaper archives, 1868-1921

GenealogyBank.com :
http://www.genealogybank.com/gbnk/newspapers/explore/USA/Wyoming/

The Online Books Page – links to historical Wyoming books and periodicals available for viewing online

The Online Books Page: http://onlinebooks.library.upenn.edu

Library of Congress Digital Newspaper Directory – free searchable database of historical U.S. newspapers dating from 1690-present

Library of Congress Digital Newspaper Directory:
http://chroniclingamerica.loc.gov/search/titles/

NewspaperArchive.com – largest online database of historical newspapers in the world.

NewspaperArchive.com: http://newspaperarchive.com/

Historical Wyoming Maps and Gazetteers

Maps are an integral part of genealogical research. They help us to
locate landmarks, towns, cities, parishes, states, provinces,
waterways and roads and streets. They also help us to determine
when and where boundary changes might have taken place, and give
us a visualization of the area we're researching in.

For locating place names, a gazetteer is the best possible resource for
any genealogist. Gazetteers are also sometimes called "place name
dictionaries", and can help you to locate the area in which you need
to conduct research. Below are links to the maps and gazetteers for
research in Wyoming.

Peabody GNIS Service – Wyoming;
http://peabody.research.yale.edu/cgi-
bin/Query.GNIS?ST=Wyoming&SU=1

Color Landform Atlas – Wyoming:
http://fermi.jhuapl.edu/states/wy_0.html

1985 U.S. Atlas link to: http://www.livgenmi.com/1895/WY/

Wyoming Hometown Locator:
http://wyoming.hometownlocator.com/

Wyoming City Directories

City directories are similar to telephone directories in that they list the residents of a particular area. The difference though is what is important to genealogists, and that is they pre-date telephone directories. You can find an ancestor's information such as their street address, place of employment, occupation, or the name of their spouse. A one-stop-shop for finding city directories in Wyoming is the **Wyoming Online Historical Directories** which contains a listing of every available online historical directory related to Wyoming. Another useful site is **US City Directories** which identifies printed, microfilmed, and online Wyoming directories and their repositories.

Wyoming Online Historical Directories:
https://sites.google.com/site/onlinedirectorysite/Home/usa/wy

US City Directories: http://www.uscitydirectories.com/wy.htm

Wyoming Genealogical Records

<u>Birth, Death, Marriage and Divorce Records</u> – Also known as vital records, birth, death, and marriage certificates are the most basic, yet most important records attached to your ancestor. The reason for their importance is that they not only place your ancestor in a specific place at a definite time, but potentially connect the individual to other relatives. Below is a list of repositories and websites where you can find Wyoming vital records.

Wyoming Department of Health – Births 1913 – present, Marriage, Divorce, and Deaths, 1963 - present

Vital Records Services
Hathaway Bldg
Cheyenne, WY 82002
Phone: 307-777-7591

Wyoming Department of Health : http://www.health.wyo.gov/

Wyoming State Archives – Birth Certificates 1909-1912, Marriage Certificates 1941-1962, county marriage record books and indexes from 1869 up to the 1960s, Divorce Certificates 1941-1962, Death Certificates 1909-1962

2301 Central Avenue
Cheyenne, WY 82002
Telephone: 307-777-7826
Fax: 307-777-7044

Wyoming State Archives:
http://wyoarchives.state.wy.us/Archives/Genealogical.aspx

Family Search has the following index that can be searched online for free:

Wyoming, Marriages, 1877-1920:
https://familysearch.org/search/collection/1708702

Census Records

Census records are among the most important genealogical documents for placing your ancestor in a particular place at a specific time. Like BDM records, they can also lead you to other ancestors, particularly those who were living under the authority of the head of household.

Wyoming State Archives – Territorial Census Records, 1869, 1875 and 1885; US Federal Census Records 1870, 1880, 1900, 1910, 1920 and 1930

2301 Central Avenue
Cheyenne, WY 82002
Telephone: 307-777-7826
Fax: 307-777-7044

Wyoming State Archives:
http://wyoarchives.state.wy.us/Archives/Genealogical.aspx

Laramie County Library – State and federal census records

2200 Pioneer Avenue
Cheyenne, WY 82001
Telephone: 307-634-3561
Fax: 307-634-2082
Genealogy & Special Collections: 307-773-7232

Laramie County Library: http://www.lclsonline.org/

National Archives at Denver - Federal population censuses for all States, 1790-1930, Indian censuses

17101 Huron Street
Broomfield, CO 80023
Telephone: 303-604-4740
Fax: 303-407-5707

National Archives at Denver:
http://www.archives.gov/denver/public/genealogy.html

The **Free Census Project** has transcribed many Wyoming indexes and new material is added daily

Free Census Project: http://usgwcensus.org/cenfiles/wy.htm

Access Genealogy – Wyoming county census records dating from 1790-1930

Access Genealogy: http://www.accessgenealogy.com/census/wyoming-census-records.htm

African American Census Schedules Online – slave schedules, mortality schedules, slave-owners census

African American Census Schedules Online: http://www.afrigeneas.com/aacensus/

Native Americans in Census Records (US National Archives): http://www.archives.gov/research/census/native-americans/

Wyoming Church Records

Church and synagogue records are a valuable resource, especially for baptisms, marriages, and burials that took place before 1900. You will need to at least have an idea of your ancestor's religious denomination, and in most cases you will have to visit a brick and mortar establishment to view them.

Most church records are kept by the individual church, although in some denominations, records are placed in a regional archive or maintained at the diocesan level. Local Historical Societies are sometimes the repository for the state's older church records. Below are links archives that maintain church records, as well as a few databases that can be viewed online.

The **Family History Library** contains many church records from a variety of denominations on microfilm.
Family History Library:
http://familysearch.org/learn/wiki/en/Family_History_Library

Central Repositories for Denominational Records

Church of Jesus Christ of Latter-day Saints (Mormons)

Early Mormon Church records for Wyoming can be found on film located at the LDS Family History Library in Salt Lake City and can be searched via the **Family History Library Catalog**

Family History Library Catalog :
https://familysearch.org/eng/Library/FHLC/frameset_fhlc.asp

The **Church History Library** has an even broader collection of historical church records than the Family History Library.
Church History Library
15 East North Temple
Salt Lake City, Utah 84150-1600
Phone: (801) 240-2272

Church History Library:
https://history.lds.org/?lang=eng#FlashPluginDetected

Baptist

American Baptist - Samuel Colgate Historical Library
1106 South Goodman Street
Rochester, NY 14620-2532
Phone: (716) 473-1740
Fax: (716) 473-1740
American Baptist - Samuel Colgate Historical Library:
http://abhsarchives.org/

Methodist

United Methodist Archives Center
Drew University Library
P.O. Box 127
Madison, NJ 07940
Phone: (201) 408-3189
Fax: (201) 408-3909
United Methodist Archives Center:
http://www.drew.edu/library/methodist

Presbyterian

Presbyterian Historical Society
425 Lombard Street
Philadelphia, PA 19147
Telephone: 1-215-627-1852
Fax: 1-215-627-0509
Presbyterian Historical Society: http://www.history.pcusa.org/

Roman Catholic

Diocese of Cheyenne
2121 Capitol Avenue
Cheyenne, WY 82001
Phone: (307) 638-1530
Fax: (307) 637-7936
Diocese of Cheyenne: http://www.dioceseofcheyenne.org/

Wyoming Military Records

More than 40 million Americans have participated in some kind of war service since America was colonized. The chance of finding your ancestor amongst those records is exceptionally high. Military records can even reveal individuals who never actually served, such as those who registered for the two World Wars but were never called to duty.

Below are a number of links to websites and archives that contain Wyoming military records.

Wyoming State Archives – Wyoming casualty lists (KIA) for WWI, WWII, and Vietnam, Spanish American War Regiment Rosters, 1890 Federal Census veterans & widows schedule, Wyoming Territorial military post returns

2301 Central Avenue
Cheyenne, WY 82002
Telephone: 307-777-7826
Fax: 307-777-7044

Wyoming State Archives:
http://wyoarchives.state.wy.us/Archives/Genealogical.aspx

National Archives at Denver – 1790-1930, Revolutionary War records, Pension and bounty land warrant applications

17101 Huron Street
Broomfield, CO 80023
Telephone: 303-604-4740
Fax: 303-407-5707

National Archives at Denver:
http://www.archives.gov/denver/public/genealogy.html

National Archives and Records Administration - World War I
Draft Registration Cards
Microfilm Roll List

8601 Adelphi Road
College Park, MD 20740-6001
Toll free: 1-866-272-6272

National Archives and Records Administration:
http://www.archives.gov/research/military/

**US Department of Veterans Affairs Nationwide Gravesite
Locator** – includes information on veterans and their family
members buried in veterans and military cemeteries having a
government grave marker.

**US Department of Veterans Affairs Nationwide Gravesite
Locator**: http://gravelocator.cem.va.gov/

You may also find your ancestor's military records in the following
databases:

United States General Index to Pension Files, 1861-1934:
https://familysearch.org/search/collection/1919699

United States Index to Service Records, War with Spain, 1898:
https://familysearch.org/search/collection/1919583

United States Index to Indian Wars Pension Files, 1892-1926 –
military pension records of soldiers who fought in the Indian Wars
between 1817 and 1898

United States Index to Indian Wars Pension Files, 1892-1926:
https://familysearch.org/search/collection/1979427

United States Registers of Enlistments in the U.S. Army, 1798-1914 - index of men who enlisted in the United States Army, 1798-1914.

United States Registers of Enlistments in the U.S. Army, 1798-1914: https://familysearch.org/search/collection/1880762

United States Mexican War Pension Index, 1887-1926 - index to Mexican War pension files for service between 1846 and 1848

United States Mexican War Pension Index, 1887-1926: https://familysearch.org/search/collection/1979390

Civil War Soldiers Service Records - Service records for both Union and Confederate soldiers indexed by soldier's name, rank, and unit.

Civil War Soldier Service Records: http://go.fold3.com/civilwar_records/

Wyoming Cemetery Records

As convenient as it is to search cemetery records online, keep in mind that there are a few disadvantages over visiting a cemetery in person. They are:

- Tombstone information is not always accurately transcribed
- The arrangement of the graves in a cemetery can be crucial as family members are often buried next to each other or in the same grave. This arrangement is not always preserved in the alphabetical indexes that are found online.

With that information in mind, the following websites have databases that can be searched online for Wyoming Cemetery records.

Wyoming Tombstone Transcription Project - death and burial records

Wyoming Tombstone Transcription Project:
http://www.usgwtombstones.org/wyoming/wyoming.html

Wyoming State Archives – Cemetery records, Wyoming cemetery survey, funeral home records

2301 Central Avenue
Cheyenne, WY 82002
Telephone: 307-777-7826
Fax: 307-777-7044

Wyoming State Archives:
http://wyoarchives.state.wy.us/Archives/Genealogical.aspx

African American Cemeteries Online – African American, slave, and Native American cemetery records

African American Cemeteries Online:
http://africanamericancemeteries.com/

Access Genealogy – database of Wyoming cemetery record transcriptions

Access Genealogy:
http://www.accessgenealogy.com/cemetery/wyoming-cemetery-records.htm

Find a Grave – over 100 million grave records can be searched on this site. Search can be conducted by name, location, or cemetery name.

Find a Grave: http://www.findagrave.com/

Interment.net - A free online database containing approximately 4 million cemetery records from around the world.

Interment.net: http://www.interment.net/

Billion Graves – as the name implies, you can search a billion records including headstone photos, transcriptions, cemetery records, and grave locations.

Billion Graves:
http://billiongraves.com/pages/search/index.php#cemetery

Wyoming Obituaries

Obituaries can reveal a wealth about our ancestor and other relatives. You can search our **Wyoming Obituaries Listings** from hundreds of Wyoming newspapers online for free.

Wyoming Obituaries Listings:
http://obituarieshelp.org/wyoming_newspaper_obituaries.html

Wyoming Wills and Probate Records

The documents found in a probate packet may include a complete inventory of a person's estate, newspaper entries, witness testimony, a copy of a will, list of debtors and creditors, names of executors or trustees, names of heirs. They can not only tell you about the ancestor you're currently researching, but lead to other ancestors.

Probate files may include a person's will, date of death, heirs, list of property and assets, and information about the settlement and distribution of the estate. As with other court records, many courts regularly transfer their inactive files to State Archives but retain their indexes. If you can't find the Wyoming probate record you're looking for in the state Archives, contact the Wyoming **Clerk of District Court** in the county the person lived in at the time of their death for a docket number
Clerk of District Court
http://www.courts.state.wy.us/DistrictCourtDirectory.aspx

Wyoming State Archives – County Clerk Land Abstracts and Deeds, Wills, and Probate records dating from late 19th century

2301 Central Avenue
Cheyenne, WY 82002
Telephone: 307-777-7826
Fax: 307-777-7044

Wyoming State Archives:
http://wyoarchives.state.wy.us/Archives/Genealogical.aspx

Laramie County Library – County probate records from Laramie and surrounding counties

2200 Pioneer Avenue
Cheyenne, WY 82001
Telephone: 307-634-3561
Fax: 307-634-2082
Genealogy & Special Collections: 307-773-7232

Laramie County Library: http://www.lclsonline.org/

Wyoming Immigration and Naturalization Records

The naturalization process generated many types of records, including petitions, declarations of intention, and oaths of allegiance. These records can provide family historians with information such as a person's birth date and place of birth, immigration year, marital status, spouse information, occupation, witnesses' names and addresses, and more.

If your ancestor lived in or near a large city, or near a city where U.S. courts convened, you may find naturalization records in the **U.S. District Court** before 1906.

U.S. District Court:
http://www.uscourts.gov/FederalCourts/UnderstandingtheFederalCourts/DistrictCourts.aspx

Laramie County Library - Wyoming Naturalization Index for the years 1867 - 1920

2200 Pioneer Avenue
Cheyenne, WY 82001
Telephone: 307-634-3561
Fax: 307-634-2082
Genealogy & Special Collections: 307-773-7232

Laramie County Library: http://www.lclsonline.org/

National Archives at Denver – Ship's Passenger lists

17101 Huron Street
Broomfield, CO 80023
Telephone: 303-604-4740
Fax: 303-407-5707

National Archives at Denver:
http://www.archives.gov/denver/public/genealogy.html

Wyoming State Archives – County naturalization records dating from the late 19th century

2301 Central Avenue
Cheyenne, WY 82002
Telephone: 307-777-7826
Fax: 307-777-7044

Wyoming State Archives:
http://wyoarchives.state.wy.us/Archives/Genealogical.aspx

US National Archives – Immigration records, Naturalization records, Ship's Passenger lists

The National Archives and Records Administration
8601 Adelphi Road
College Park, MD 20740-6001
Tel: 1-866-272-6272; 1-86-NARA-NARAS

US National Archives: http://www.archives.gov/research/guide-fed-records/groups/085.html

Wyoming Native American Records

Wyoming Memory (Digital Archive) – Plains Indian Museum Collections Database

Wyoming Memory: http://www.wyomingmemory.org/history.htm

Fold3 (Digital Archive) – Indian Census Rolls, Dawes Packets, Dawes Enrolment Cards, and moreCherokee Applications,

Fold3: http://go.fold3.com/native_americans_records/

Marquette University - Records of St. Stephen's Mission Wyoming, dating from 1880's; records of the Tekakwitha Conference (Minnesota, Montana, North Dakota, South Dakota and Wyoming, 1939-1970s)

Department of Special Collections and University Archives
R360 John P. Raynor, S.J., Library
1355 W. Wisconsin Ave.
Milwaukee, Wisconsin 53233
Telephone: (414) 288-5904
Fax: (414) 288-6709
mark.thiel@marquette.edu

Mailing Address:

Raynor Memorial Libraries
P.O. Box 3141
Milwaukee, Wisconsin 53201-3141

Department of Special Collections and University Archives:
http://www.marquette.edu/library/archives/indians.shtml

National Archives at Denver – Native American censuses

17101 Huron Street
Broomfield, CO 80023
Telephone: 303-604-4740
Fax: 303-407-5707

National Archives at Denver:
http://www.archives.gov/denver/public/genealogy.html

National Archives and Records Administration - Dawes
Commission Final Cards of the Five Civilized Tribes

8601 Adelphi Road
College Park, MD 20740-6001
Toll free: 1-866-272-6272

National Archives and Records Administration:
http://www.archives.gov/research/military/

Access Genealogy – Wyoming Native American census records,
tribal histories, and much more

Access Genealogy:
http://www.accessgenealogy.com/native/wyoming-indian-tribes.htm

U.S. National Archives - information on American Indians who
maintained their ties to Federally-recognized Tribes (1830-1970).

U.S. National Archives: http://www.archives.gov/research/native-
americans/

Records of the Bureau of Indian Affairs (BIA):
http://www.archives.gov/research/guide-fed-
records/groups/075.html

American Indians Records Repository - records dating from the 1700s including trust, education and other historic Indian Affairs records

American Indian Records Repository
Meritex Enterprises
17501 West 98th Street
Lenexa, KS 66219
Phone: 913-888-0601

American Indians Records Repository:
http://www.doi.gov/ost/records_mgmt/american-indian-records-repository.cfm

Missing Matriarchs – Resources for Researching Female Wyoming Ancestors

Looking for female ancestors requires an adjustment of how we view traditional records sources. A woman's identity was often under that of her husband, and often individual records for them can be difficult to locate. The following resources are effective in locating female ancestors in Wyoming where traditional records may not reveal them.

Bibliographies

- *Wyoming from Territorial Days to Present. 3 Vols.,* Frances B. Beard (American History Society, 1933)
- *The Important Things of Life: Women, Work, and Family in Sweetwater County, Wyoming, 1880-1929,* Dee Garceau (Putnam's Sons, 1958)
- *The Feminine Frontier: Wyoming Women, 1850-1900,* Denice Wheeler (The Author, 1987)
- *Stories of Early Days in Wyoming: Big Horn Basin,* Tacetta B. Walker (Daily Sentinel Print, 1875)

Selected Resources for Wyoming Women's History

Women's History Research Center
American Heritage Center
University of Wyoming
Box 3924
Laramie, WY 82071-3924

Laramie County Library
2200 Pioneer Avenue
Cheyenne, WY 82001

Wyoming State Archives
2301 Central Avenue
Cheyenne, WY 82002

Common Wyoming Surnames

The following surnames are among the most common in Wyoming and are also being currently researched by other genealogists. If you find your surname here, there is a chance that some research has already been performed on your ancestor.

Abraham, Appleby, Andrus, Barone, Baroody, Bates, Battermann, Baughman, Berry, Beissner, Binning, Bloomfield, Bowers, Bowman, Boynton, Bradshaw, Brady, Brown, Brunel, Buchmeier, Burbeck, Camp, Campbell, Carter, Cater, Chiester, Christiansen, Churchill, Clements, Coffta, Coggins, Colshan, Combs, Conyers, Cottle, Crawford, Dahlsted, Danhuaser, Darling, Davis, Delp, DeRosa, Dickinson, Dixon, Doman, Douglas, Dupaly, Dye, Draeger, Eastin, Ellis, Engelking, Engel, Erickson, Estep, Evans, Ezquierdo, Fergus, Fisher, Froman, Fuller, Fowler, Fry, Frye, Gardner, Gaveka, Garcia, Gawel, Generous, Gerland, Gewecke, Georgeanna, Gersbach, Glasgow, Gongwer, Greser, Gulli, Gustin, Hagerdon, Hall, Hasenjaeger, Hammer, Hancy, Heishman, Helsley, Heltzel, Hendrickson, Hively, Herendeen, Hines, Hoag, Holsow, Holt, Holmes, Houghton, Hunter, Hurt, Huxhold, Huxhole, Huzzy, Hyatt, Issa, Jackson, James, Jenkins, Jepson, Johnston,Johnson, Joseph, Justus, Karcher, Kauke, Kelkenberg, Keller, Kendell, Kimball, King, Kirkley, Knight, Korecko, Krause, Khour, King, Kirchoff, Koch, Koehler, Kossuth, Krama, Laird, Lange, Lawless, Lewis, Lomax, Long, Lemons, Leybe, Lien, Loghry, Lowther, Luther, Magdalena, Martinez, Maynard, Merk, Matthies, McCoy, Merckel, Meriwether, Merkele, Meyer, Micheal, Mills, Moeller, Morgan, Moomaw, Moore, Morris, Mullins, Munson, Nation, Neese, Neels, Nicholaus, Nowatzki, O'Leary, Offutt, Ostfeld, Owen, Oxford, Olson, Orndorff, Ovis, Parent, Pasquali, Pape, Parmalee, Partley, Payne, Peachy, Peasley, Petet, Peterson, Pitman, Pohler, Pope, Potts, Preckel, Quarles, Ramaha, Ranney, Reade, Rice, Riding, Richardson, Roberts, Roberta, Robertson, Rogers, Rosenbaum, Ross, Sager, Sale, Sanchez, Santucci, Schamber, Scott, Schaper, Scranton, Senne, Seegers, Seggebrok, Sieckmann, Shadman, Shanley, Showman/Sherman, Smith, Spair, Spereaw, Spears, Stahlhut, Stunkel, Swift, Spigle, Spillman, Stevens, Stipke,

Tanner, Taliaferro, Taylor, Tegtmeier, Thatcher, Thomas, Thorton, Thurlow, Thyret, Tindell, Tussing, Umberger, Van Male, Vandehei, VanLeuven, Vehling, Veach, Wakefield, Walker, Warner, Warnstrom, Webster, Wetzel, Whitman, Wicken, Wilcox, Wilson, Wilkenson, Wilkins, Willard, Woodhouse, Wright

About the Author

Gary L. Morris worked from 2009 to 2014 as a professional researcher for a major player in the genealogy field. After tracing his family lineage back to 1683, he found that genealogy could be an expensive undertaking. As such, has decided to publish these helpful guides to share the valuable free information he has discovered during his career to help others trace their family lineages as inexpensively as possible. An avid genealogist himself, he hopes you will find this guide factual, thorough, helpful, and most of all, effective in helping you to find your family members.

Notes

Notes

www.ingramcontent.com/pod-product-compliance
Lightning Source LLC
Chambersburg PA
CBHW070512290526
45790CB00003B/1207